I0820964

INSIDE THE NFL

MINNESOTA VIKINGS

by Charlie Beattie

Abdo & Daughters
MIDDLE GRADE NONFICTION
An imprint of Abdo Publishing
abdobooks.com

Published by Abdo Publishing, a division of ABDO, PO Box 398166, Minneapolis, Minnesota 55439.

Printed in China.
052025
092025

THIS BOOK CONTAINS RECYCLED MATERIALS

Cover Photos: David Berding/Getty Images Sport/Getty Images (Justin Jefferson); Sporting News/Getty Images (Randy Moss)
Interior Photos: Stephen Maturen/Getty Images Sport/Getty Images, 4–5, 7, 8; Steph Chambers/Getty Images Sport/Getty Images, 6; Mike Mulholland/Getty Images Sport/Getty Images, 9, 61 (bottom right); Abdo Publishing, 10–11; R. H. Finn/AP Images, 12–13; David Durochik/AP Images, 14, 20; AP Images, 15, 18, 28, 60 (bottom left), 60 (bottom right); San Francisco Examiner/AP Images, 16; Focus on Sport/Getty Images, 17, 26, 32, 33; Tony Tomsic/AP Images, 19, 23, 60 (top); Vernon Biever/AP Images, 21, 29; James Flores/Getty Images Sport/Getty Images, 24–25; JT/AP Images, 27; JM/AP Images, 31; George Rose/Getty Images Sport/Getty Images, 34–35; Focus on Sport/Getty Images Sport/Getty Images, 36; Eric Risberg/AP Images, 37; Michael J. Minardi/Getty Images Sport/Getty Images, 38; Jerry Holt/Star Tribune/Getty Images, 39, 43, 53, 61 (bottom left); Al Messerschmidt Archive/AP Images, 40; Tom Olmscheid/AP Images, 41; Gin Ellis/Getty Images Sport/Getty Images, 42; Tim Sharp/AP Images, 44; Beth A. Keiser/AP Images, 45; Tom Dahlin/Getty Images Sport/Getty Images, 46–47; Genevieve Ross/AP Images, 48, 61 (top); David Stluka/AP Images, 49; Jamie Squire/Getty Images Sport/Getty Images, 50, 56, 57; Rich Gabrielson/Icon Sport Media/Icon Sportswire/Getty Images, 51; Ann Heisenfelt/AP Images, 52; Greg Trott/AP images, 55; Hannah Foslien/Getty Images Sport/Getty Images, 54; Shutterstock Images, 58; Nick Wosika/Icon Sportswire/Getty Images, 59, 63

Editor: Arnold Ringstad
Series Designer: Laura Graphenteen
Production Designer: Ryan Gale

Library of Congress Control Number: 2024948463

Publisher's Cataloging-in-Publication Data

Names: Beattie, Charlie, author.
Title: Minnesota Vikings / by Charlie Beattie
Description: Minneapolis, Minnesota: Abdo Publishing, 2026 | Series: Inside the NFL | Includes online resources and index.
Identifiers: ISBN 9781098296827 (lib. bdg.) | ISBN 9798384919346 (ebook)
Subjects: LCSH: Minnesota Vikings (Football team)--Juvenile literature. | National Football League--Juvenile literature. | Football teams--Juvenile literature. | American football--Juvenile literature.
Classification: DDC 796.333--dc23

CONTENTS

Wide receiver Justin Jefferson runs onto the field before the Vikings' matchup with the San Francisco 49ers in Week 2 of the 2024 season.

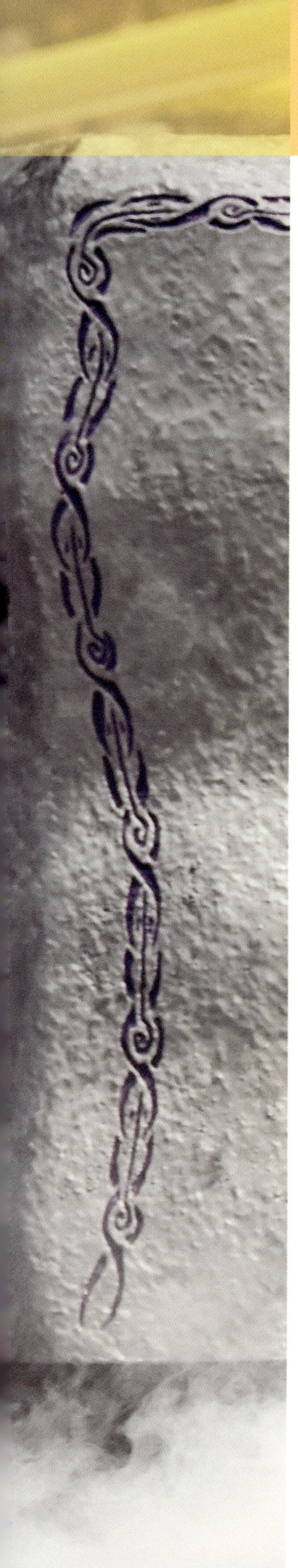

CHAPTER 1

GOING DEEP

MINNESOTA VIKINGS RECEIVER JUSTIN JEFFERSON GOT READY TO BURST off the line of scrimmage. The San Francisco 49ers wouldn't expect it. It was early in the teams' matchup during Week 2 of the 2024 National Football League (NFL) season. Minnesota was backed up to its own 3-yard line. The 49ers were the defending National Football Conference (NFC) champions and had a strong defense. Most teams wouldn't think of throwing a long pass in their own territory. But most teams didn't have Jefferson.

The lanky 6-foot-1-inch Jefferson had just begun his fifth season with the Vikings. In his first four seasons, Jefferson put up 5,899 receiving yards and had 392 receptions. No receiver in the history of the NFL had more yards in his first four years.

The talented duo of Jordan Addison, *left*, and Justin Jefferson, *right*, combined to score 19 receiving touchdowns in the 2024 season.

BREAKING AWAY

Many of Jefferson's best plays had been deep passes. In each of his first four years, he had caught at least one pass of 50 yards or more. Vikings fans at U.S. Bank Stadium in Minneapolis learned to get excited as soon as the ball was headed toward No. 18. They knew a spectacular play might happen.

That was what Vikings coach Kevin O'Connell was hoping for when he called a play-action pass on second down from his own 3-yard line. The Vikings' plan looked even more promising when 49ers safety George Odum lined up across from Jefferson.

Kevin O'Connell became the head coach of the Vikings in 2022.

Safeties aren't usually asked to cover star receivers one-on-one. That job is typically saved for the most skilled cornerbacks. Even the best safeties in the NFL struggle to stick with Jefferson.

Minnesota quarterback Sam Darnold took the snap, faked a handoff to running back Aaron Jones, then settled into the pocket. Jefferson exploded past Odum and streaked down the middle of the field. San Francisco safety Ji'Ayir Brown waited there for Jefferson. But with a subtle head fake, Jefferson sent Brown toward the sideline. Minnesota's stellar receiver then continued into the open space.

Darnold lobbed a pass that was right on target. Jefferson was 2 yards behind both Odum and Brown when he hauled in the ball at midfield. As both defenders closed in, Jefferson headed up the far sideline. Realizing that he was about to be cut off, Jefferson stopped in his tracks. Both Odum and Brown flew past him. As more than 60,000 fans exploded in cheers, Jefferson reversed back

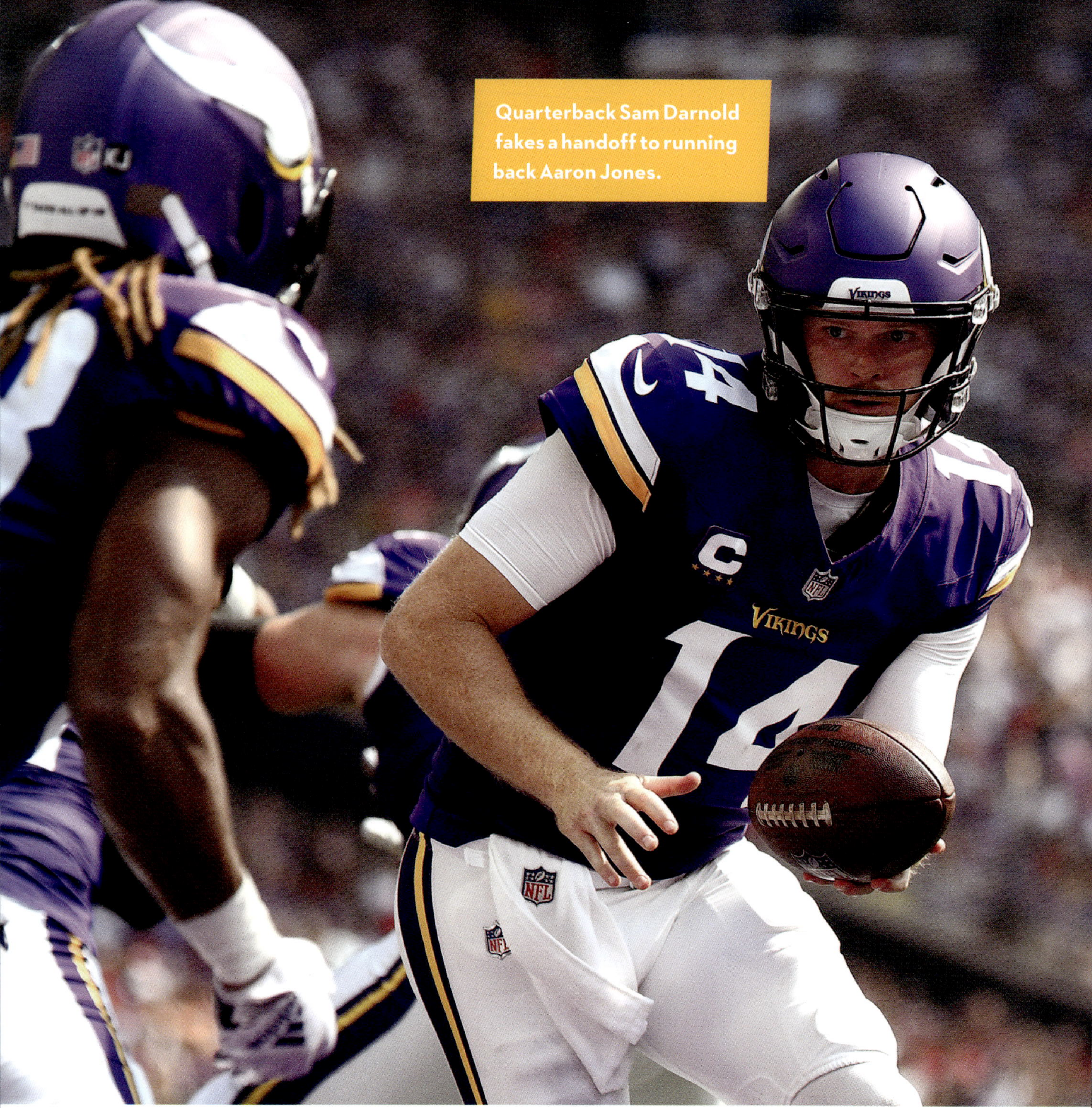

Quarterback Sam Darnold fakes a handoff to running back Aaron Jones.

"WHEN [JEFFERSON] CUT BACK, THAT'S WHEN I KIND OF KNEW WE WERE GOING TO SCORE."

—SAM DARNOLD

toward the other side of the field. "When he cut back, that's when I kind of knew we were going to score," Darnold said after the game.

NEARLY A RECORD

Jefferson angled toward the pylon at the corner of the end zone. Fellow receiver Jalen Nailor, who sprinted the length of the field, threw a key block to clear Jefferson's path. Jefferson reached for the purple-painted end zone just before the defense could angle him out of bounds.

It was by far the longest reception of Jefferson's already thrilling career. The 97-yard passing play fell just 2 yards short of the team record. But that didn't matter to the crowd at U.S. Bank Stadium. Jefferson's incredible catch and run put the Vikings up 10–0 on their way to a 23–17 victory. The 25-year-old star receiver finished the day with four catches for 133 yards and one touchdown. But it was just another game for a player who could seemingly do anything on a football field.

A LONG WAY TO GO

In 2014, the NFL began tracking advanced player statistics, such as running speed and distance covered. According to the league's system, Justin Jefferson reached nearly 20 miles per hour (32 km/h) on his 97-yard touchdown. And because he sprinted across the field twice, Jefferson actually covered 127 1/2 yards before finally scoring.

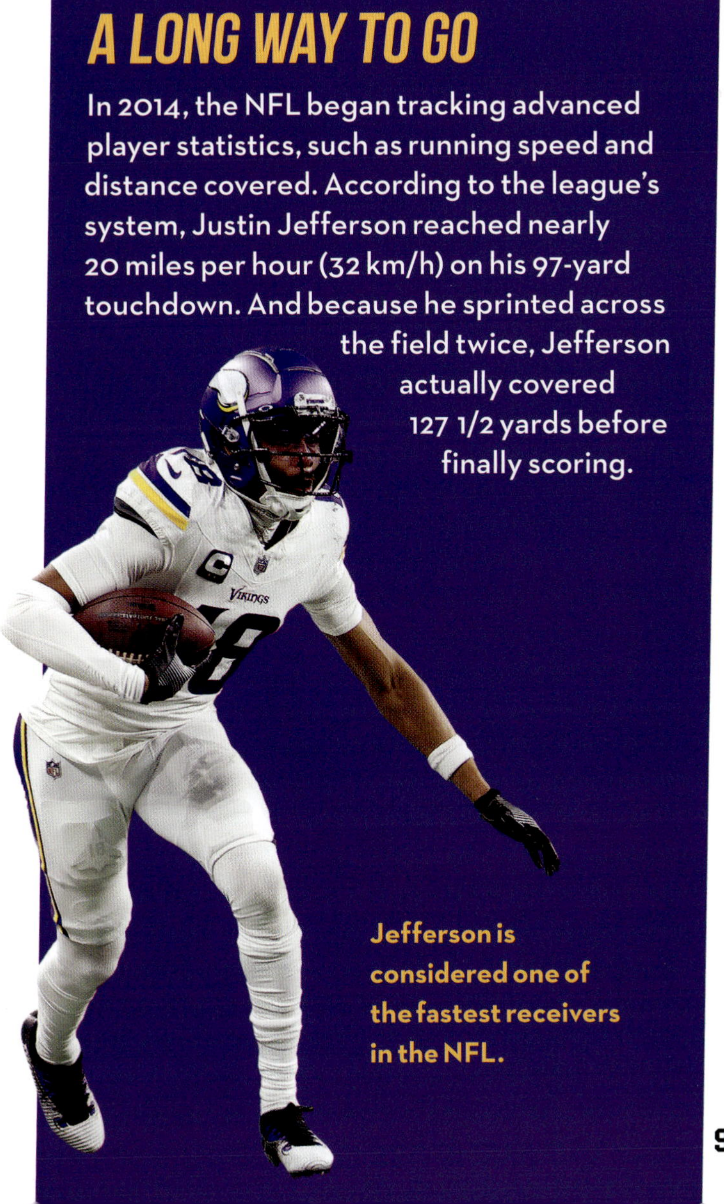

Jefferson is considered one of the fastest receivers in the NFL.

NFL TEAMS MAP

NFC EAST

NFC WEST

NFC NORTH

NFC SOUTH

AFC

AFC EAST

- BUFFALO BILLS
- MIAMI DOLPHINS
- NEW ENGLAND PATRIOTS
- NEW YORK JETS

AFC WEST

- DENVER BRONCOS
- KANSAS CITY CHIEFS
- LAS VEGAS RAIDERS
- LOS ANGELES CHARGERS

AFC NORTH

- BALTIMORE RAVENS
- CINCINNATI BENGALS
- CLEVELAND BROWNS
- PITTSBURGH STEELERS

AFC SOUTH

- HOUSTON TEXANS
- INDIANAPOLIS COLTS
- JACKSONVILLE JAGUARS
- TENNESSEE TITANS

NFL commissioner Pete Rozelle, *left*, and Vikings general manager Bert Rose, *right*, pose with a season ticket holder before the team's first season in 1961.

CHAPTER 2

VIKING LEGENDS

IN 1959, THE STATE OF MINNESOTA FOUND ITSELF IN THE MIDDLE OF A professional football war. The sport was surging in popularity. The NFL wanted to add new teams. Meanwhile, the rival American Football League (AFL) was starting up to challenge the older NFL.

Led by businessman Max Winter, a local ownership group signed on with the AFL in August 1959. The league was set to begin play less than a year later. But in January 1960, the NFL came along with a better offer. So, Winter and his partners swapped leagues.

The team was set to begin play in 1961, giving the owners an extra year to prepare. One key decision was coming up with a name. General manager Bert Rose suggested they call the team the Vikings. It worked for the football team, the

Defensive end Jim Marshall served as the Vikings' team captain from 1966 to 1979.

owners reasoned, because Minnesota has a large population of Scandinavian Americans.

Rose also hired retired NFL quarterback Norm Van Brocklin as head coach and put together the team's first roster. By the time the Vikings took the field, Rose had already signed a handful of players destined for memorable careers in the team's purple-and-gold uniforms. One of Rose's best early moves was trading with the Cleveland Browns for Jim Marshall. The defensive end became a key member of what would develop into a strong defense in Minnesota. He spent 19 years with the Vikings and appeared in a then-record 282 consecutive games.

With their first draft pick, the Vikings selected running back Tommy Mason. The fleet-footed Mason admitted that he ran quickly because he was playing scared. But no matter how he felt, Mason surged for 28 rushing touchdowns and scored another 11 through the air in six years as a Viking.

SCRAMBLIN' FRAN

Playing in front of Mason was a skinny, athletic quarterback from Georgia named Fran Tarkenton. He was Minnesota's third-round pick in 1961. At first, Tarkenton played like most quarterbacks of the day. He stood in the pocket and rarely ran. But after the Chicago Bears pummeled him in a 1961 preseason game, Tarkenton knew he had to change his ways.

Quarterback Fran Tarkenton races away from a Green Bay Packers defender during a game in 1966.

The 6-foot, 190-pound player became football's premier running quarterback. Not only did he pick up yardage, but "Scramblin' Fran" made a Hall of Fame career out of zigzagging behind the line of scrimmage and running away from opposing pass rushers until a receiver came open.

Tarkenton showed Minnesota fans an early taste of his game in the season opener against those same Bears. The rookie didn't start, but Van Brocklin inserted Tarkenton midway through the first quarter. Tarkenton finished the game with four touchdown passes, plus another on the ground. The Vikings shocked the powerful Bears 37–13. No other NFL expansion team would win its opening game for 41 years.

Despite the great start, the Vikings struggled to win games early. They finished 1961 just 3–11. Minnesota didn't have a winning year until 1964, but throughout the decade the Vikings continued to add players who would become the core of a contending team. No team took center Mick Tingelhoff in any of the 20 rounds in the 1962 draft. The Vikings signed him as a free agent. He became an instant starter and held the job for 17 years on his way to the Hall of Fame.

JIM MARSHALL'S WRONG-WAY RUN

In a 1964 matchup with the San Francisco 49ers, the Vikings led 27–17 in the fourth quarter. Jim Marshall scooped up a fumble at the San Francisco 34-yard line. He then sprinted 66 yards into the wrong end zone, accidentally scoring a safety for the 49ers. In the end, Marshall's mistake didn't hurt Minnesota. The team won 27–22, and the winning touchdown had come after Marshall caused a fumble that teammate Carl Eller ran into the correct end zone.

Jim Marshall scoops up the fumble on his way to the wrong end zone in 1964.

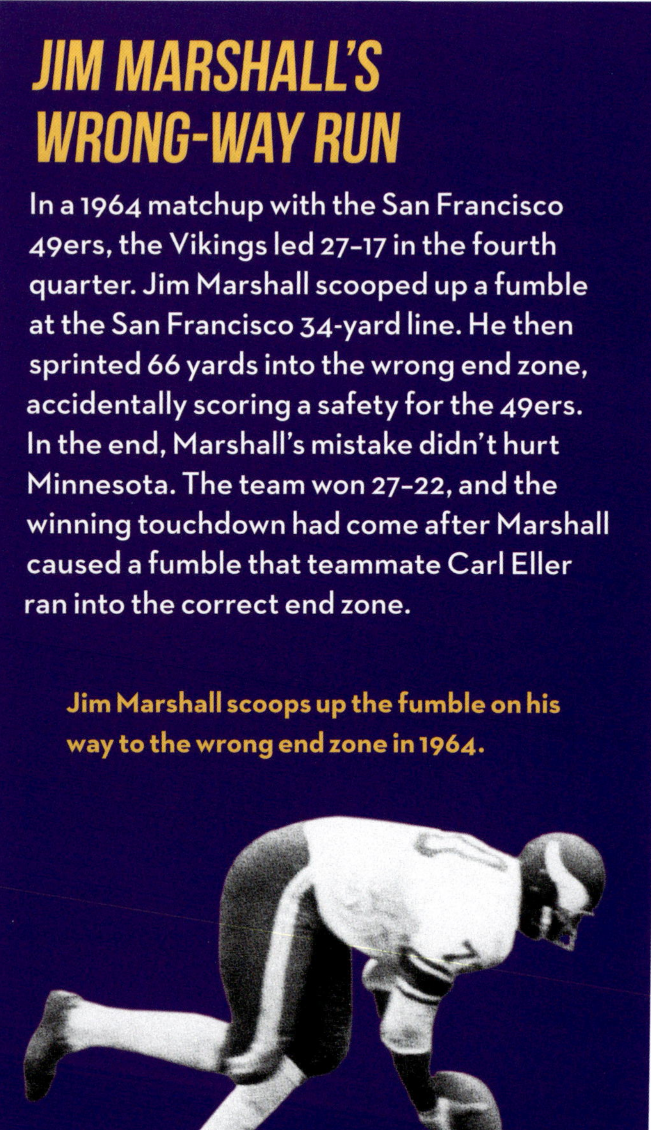

Defensive end Carl Eller was named to the Pro Bowl six times between 1968 and 1974.

Minnesota drafted standout defensive end Carl Eller in 1964. He and Marshall became the bookends of Minnesota's fearsome front four. The team added versatile running back Dave Osborn in the 13th round of the 1965 draft.

NORTH OF THE BORDER

By 1966, the Vikings had plenty of talent, but most of those players clashed with Van Brocklin. The coach didn't like Tarkenton's scrambling and spent years trying to rein in his star player. Tarkenton grew fed up and asked for a trade. Van Brocklin surprisingly quit in February 1967. A month later, new general manager Jim Finks shipped Tarkenton to the New York Giants.

The Vikings now needed a new coach and a new quarterback. Finks had joined the Vikings in 1964 from the Canadian Football League (CFL). He looked north to find the solution to his problems. Bud Grant had initially turned down the head coaching job with the

Vikings in 1961 to stay with the CFL's Winnipeg Blue Bombers. But when Finks came calling, Grant signed on. Grant was a stern, disciplined head coach. He was also very familiar with Minnesota. The Wisconsin native had played college football and basketball at the University of Minnesota, as well as pro basketball for the Minneapolis Lakers.

Bud Grant had a record of 158-96-5 during his 18 seasons as Minnesota's head coach.

Finks and Grant picked up another CFL player to take over under center. Quarterback Joe Kapp didn't have Tarkenton's arm or scrambling ability, but he displayed toughness and tremendous leadership. Though Minnesota won only three games in 1967, Grant and Kapp quickly turned the Vikings around. It didn't hurt that Finks had an eye for Hall of Fame talent. He traded for safety Paul Krause in 1968. The ball hawk went on to become the NFL's all-time interceptions leader. In that year's draft, the Vikings picked up offensive tackle Ron Yary in the first round. A year earlier, Minnesota had selected talented defensive tackle Alan Page.

Safety Paul Krause finished his career with an NFL-record 81 interceptions. He recorded 53 of them as a Viking.

40 FOR 60

By 1968, Grant's Vikings had become a force. The team went 8-6 and reached the playoffs for the first time before losing 24-14 to the Baltimore Colts. A year later, the Vikings got a chance for revenge. In a Week 2 matchup against the Colts, Kapp threw an NFL-record-tying seven touchdown passes in a lopsided 52-14 victory.

Offensive tackle Ron Yary made six All-Pro teams as a member of the Vikings between 1968 and 1981.

Minnesota's offense continued to light up scoreboards in 1969 and led the league in scoring. The defense, featuring Krause, Eller, Marshall, Page, and Pro Bowl defensive tackle Gary Larsen, allowed only 133 points in 14 games. That mark was the lowest total in the NFL since 1946.

Despite the great statistics, the biggest reason for Minnesota's 12-2 record in 1969 was its spirit of togetherness. The team bonded around the slogan "40 for 60." At the time, NFL rosters were limited to 40 players. The slogan meant that all 40 Vikings had to give

Quarterback Joe Kapp threw 37 touchdown passes and rushed for five more touchdowns during his three seasons with the Vikings.

everything they had for 60 minutes. At a team banquet at the end of the year, the Vikings named Kapp their Most Valuable Player (MVP). He took the stage and said, "There is no Most Valuable Viking. There are 40 Most Valuable Vikings. 40 for 60, put it that way. I just can't accept this."

"THERE IS NO MOST VALUABLE VIKING. THERE ARE 40 MOST VALUABLE VIKINGS."

—JOE KAPP

Minnesota put that camaraderie on full display in the playoffs. In the opening round, the Vikings hosted the Los Angeles Rams on a frozen field at

Metropolitan Stadium in Bloomington, Minnesota. The Vikings fell behind 17–7 at the half. But Kapp sealed a comeback win in the fourth quarter. First, he hit receiver Gene Washington on a long pass play to get near the goal line. Kapp then put Minnesota up 21–20 by running in a 2-yard score. Minnesota later added two points with a safety. Page sealed the 23–20 win with an interception.

That put the Vikings in the NFL Championship Game against the Browns. Early in the game, Kapp turned to hand off but collided with his running back. The quick-thinking quarterback held on to the ball and barreled into the end zone for a 7–0 lead. Later in the first quarter, he lobbed a pass to a wide-open Washington down the middle of the field. Minnesota's top receiver raced 75 yards for a score. The Vikings eventually built a 27–0 lead before winning 27–7.

Though the Vikings won the NFL title, technically they were not the champions yet. Four years earlier, the league had decided to merge with the AFL. The two leagues were set to become one in 1970. In the meantime, the NFL and AFL champions met in a true championship game now known as the Super Bowl.

In Super Bowl IV, Minnesota faced the AFL champion Kansas City Chiefs. Though the Vikings came in as heavy favorites, they fell flat as Kansas City built a 16–0 first-half lead. Minnesota managed to score a touchdown in the third quarter, but Kansas City responded with a touchdown of its own, winning 23–7.

Even with the loss, the Vikings were set up with the talent to reach a championship game again. Grant's team was only going to get better. Minnesota's frozen fans just hoped the team would eventually be able to finish the job.

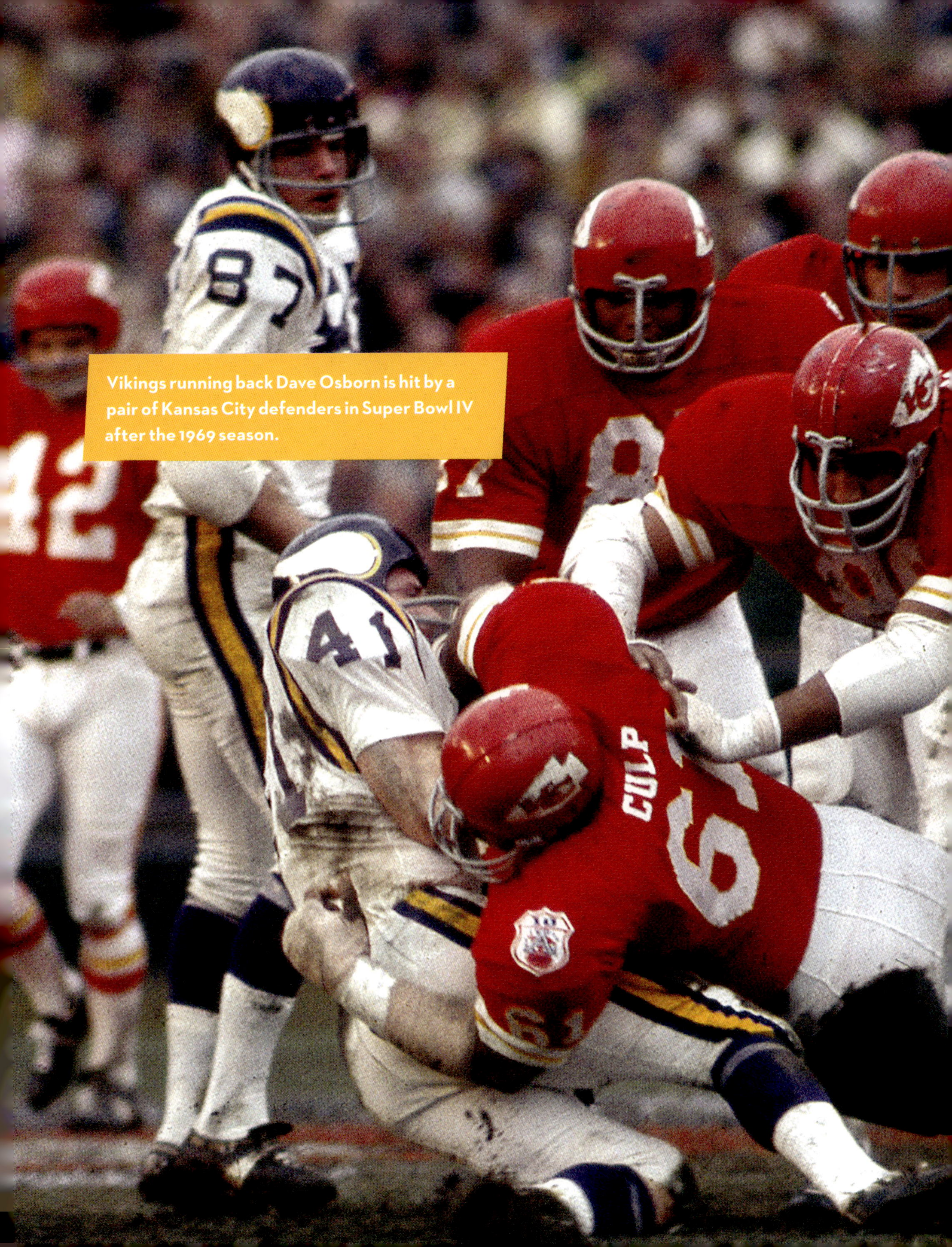

Vikings running back Dave Osborn is hit by a pair of Kansas City defenders in Super Bowl IV after the 1969 season.

From left, Jim Marshall, Carl Eller, Alan Page, and Gary Larsen formed a fearsome defensive line for the Vikings.

CHAPTER 3

THE PURPLE PEOPLE EATERS

In the 1970s, opposing offensive players feared traveling to Minnesota for games. The weather was often cold, especially late in the season, and blustery winds regularly blew through the Vikings' Metropolitan Stadium. The Vikings loved to celebrate their frozen advantage. "When the sun would drop behind the back of the stadium, the temperature would drop," said defensive end Jim Marshall. "We would, under our breath, start saying, 'Odin, Odin, Odin,' the Viking God of War."

While the chant may have been intimidating, Marshall and his defensive line partners didn't need it. They scared teams all on their own. By 1970, the line made up of ends Marshall and Carl Eller, along with tackles Gary Larsen and Alan Page, was recognized as one of the NFL's best.

Marshall served as the defensive captain. Eller, nicknamed "Moose," rushed the passer ferociously and became known for playing well in big games. Larsen was a steady force at tackle. Meanwhile, Page possessed a combination of high intelligence and elite athleticism. After his Hall of Fame career ended, he spent 22 years as a justice on Minnesota's Supreme Court.

The talented quartet picked up a catchy nickname as it dominated opponents. They were dubbed "the Purple People Eaters" after a 1958 novelty song about a one-eyed space alien. Marshall hated what he thought was a cartoonish nickname. He preferred to call his group "the Purple Gang."

Whatever people wanted to call them, the Vikings defensive front needed to be great in the early 1970s to make up for the team's struggles on offense. Quarterback Joe Kapp had left the Vikings, and replacements Gary Cuozzo, Bob Lee, and Norm Snead threw only 21 touchdown passes between 1970 and 1971. Minnesota still went 23-5 in those two seasons thanks to its mighty defense. However, the team lost its playoff opener in both years.

Tackle Alan Page was named the NFL's MVP in 1971.

A FAMILIAR FACE

Before the 1972 season, general manager Jim Finks and coach Bud Grant brought Fran Tarkenton back to Minnesota. At first, it looked like the move for the 32-year-old was a mistake. The Vikings finished just 7–7. At the 1973 draft, Finks brought in more offensive help. The team spent its first-round pick on hard-charging running back Chuck Foreman. The versatile back won the Offensive Rookie of the Year Award by piling up more than 1,100 total yards and six touchdowns. Minnesota surged back to the playoffs with a 12–2 record.

Running back Chuck Foreman left the Vikings in 1980 as the team's all-time leading rusher with 5,887 yards.

The Vikings opened the playoffs against the defending NFC champions from Washington. With the Vikings trailing 13–10 in the fourth quarter, Tarkenton took over. He threw a pair of touchdown passes to top receiver John Gilliam to lead Minnesota to a 27–20 victory.

That win set up a meeting with the Dallas Cowboys in the NFC title game. Two years earlier, Dallas had roughed up Cuozzo and Lee in the playoffs on its way to winning Super Bowl VI. The Cowboys couldn't do the same to Tarkenton. The Vikings star connected with Gilliam on a 54-yard bomb in the third quarter to put Minnesota up 17–7. Minnesota still led 17–10 early in the fourth quarter when veteran cornerback Bobby Bryant picked off Dallas's Roger Staubach near the sideline and raced 63 yards for a game-sealing score. Kicker Fred Cox added a field goal for a 27–10 victory and the NFC title.

The Vikings faced the defending champion Miami Dolphins in Super Bowl VIII. Just like Minnesota, Miami won games on the strength of a stout defense and a powerful running game.

Miami running back Larry Csonka powers through Minnesota's defense for one of his two touchdowns in Super Bowl VIII after the 1973 season.

The Dolphins' star rusher, Larry Csonka, blasted through the Purple People Eaters for a then–Super Bowl record 145 yards and a pair of touchdowns. Minnesota had no answer. The Vikings didn't score until Tarkenton scrambled for a 4-yard touchdown late in the game. By then, it was already over. Miami won 24–7.

SUPER BOWL STRUGGLES

By 1974, the Vikings had been around long enough to develop fierce rivalries. They battled twice per year with their NFC Central rivals the Detroit Lions, Green Bay Packers, and Chicago Bears. Games within the division were so hard-hitting that the NFC Central became known as "the Black and Blue Division." But in the 1970s, the purple-clad Vikings dished out most of the punishment.

The Green Bay Packers have been Minnesota's fiercest rival since the Vikings entered the NFL.

Minnesota won the division again in 1974 behind its tested combination of defense and offense. Foreman topped the NFL in touchdowns that year. After beating the St. Louis Cardinals and Los Angeles Rams in the playoffs, Minnesota became the first NFL team to reach the Super Bowl for a third time.

The Vikings' opponents in Super Bowl IX were the equally hard-hitting Pittsburgh Steelers. Pittsburgh's defensive front was known as "the Steel Curtain." On a cold, wet day in New Orleans, the Steelers froze the Vikings' offense. Minnesota managed to gain only 119 yards. Five decades later, that was still the lowest total in any Super Bowl. Minnesota's only score came on special teams. Under the detail-oriented Grant, the Vikings had always thrived at blocking kicks. Down 9–0 in the fourth quarter, Minnesota linebacker Matt Blair burst through the line and blocked a Steelers punt deep in Pittsburgh territory. The ball rolled into the end zone, where Vikings safety Terry Brown covered it. But Minnesota missed the extra-point attempt, and the Steelers scored late to win 16–6.

THE HAIL MARY

In the division playoffs after the 1975 season, the Vikings lost 17–14 to Dallas on one of football's most famous plays. Cowboys quarterback Roger Staubach hit receiver Drew Pearson on a 50-yard touchdown pass to win the game. It was one of the earliest plays described as a "Hail Mary." But the Vikings insist it should never have stood. They claim that Pearson shoved Minnesota cornerback Nate Wright to the ground before making the catch and should have been called for offensive pass interference.

END OF THE RUN

By 1976, the Vikings were known as the team that couldn't win the big game. But Minnesota put together another strong regular season, finishing 11–2–1. Tarkenton then opened the playoffs by throwing three touchdown passes in a 35–20 rout of Washington.

Vikings tight end Stu Voight scores Minnesota's opening touchdown against Washington in the 1976 playoffs.

In the NFC title game, Minnesota's stellar special teams once again stepped up. The Los Angeles Rams lined up for a short field goal in the first quarter, but the Vikings blocked it. Bryant scooped up the ball and raced for a 90-yard touchdown. The thrilling play set the tone for a 24–13 Vikings win. For the third time in four years, Minnesota earned a trip to the Super Bowl.

This time, Minnesota faced another powerhouse opponent in the Oakland Raiders. The aging Vikings struggled. Minnesota's normally stout defense couldn't contain the Raiders' running game as Oakland piled up 266 rushing yards. The Raiders took the air out of the Vikings by building a 16–0 halftime lead.

Tarkenton managed to cut the lead to 19–7 on a third-quarter touchdown pass to rookie Sammy White. But in the fourth, Tarkenton tried to sneak a pass to the left sideline. Oakland cornerback Willie Brown picked it off and sprinted 75 yards for

Vikings linebacker Jeff Siemon (50) and cornerback Nate Allen (25) try to bring down Oakland's Clarence Davis in Super Bowl XI.

a score. After that, Tarkenton came out of the game. Backup Bob Lee threw a late touchdown pass, but Minnesota lost 32–14.

The Vikings had now lost four Super Bowls, including three in a span of four years. Despite the fact that Minnesota had been one of the most dominant teams of the 1970s, the team was remembered for its failures. The losses stung the players. "We played in the big game, and we lost all three times that I quarterbacked. I have never gotten over that," Tarkenton said years later.

"WE PLAYED IN THE BIG GAME, AND WE LOST ALL THREE TIMES THAT I QUARTERBACKED. I HAVE NEVER GOTTEN OVER THAT."

—FRAN TARKENTON

The veteran Vikings were also losing their window of opportunity. Though the team reached the playoffs in both 1977 and 1978, Minnesota slowly lost its longtime stars. Tarkenton, center Mick Tingelhoff, Eller, and Page left after the 1978 season. Marshall and safety Paul Krause left after 1979. Grant remained, but he now needed to rebuild his team.

Quarterback Fran Tarkenton retired as the NFL's all-time leader in passing yards and touchdowns.

Jerry Burns joined the Vikings as the team's offensive coordinator in 1968. He held the job for 18 years before his promotion to head coach.

CHAPTER 4

DOME DOMINANCE

THE VIKINGS WENT THROUGH MANY CHANGES IN THE LATE 1970S AND early 1980s. None was bigger than a move to a new home. After 21 seasons of forcing visiting opponents to suffer through the frozen temperatures of Metropolitan Stadium, the Vikings moved indoors to the Hubert H. Humphrey Metrodome in 1982.

Bud Grant stuck around to see the Vikings change addresses but retired following the 1983 season. The coach known for his icy sideline stare was beloved by his players and Minnesota's fans. And after Grant's replacement, Les Steckel, oversaw a disastrous 3–13 season in 1984, Grant unretired. He righted Minnesota's ship in 1985, then left for good, turning the Vikings over to longtime offensive coordinator Jerry Burns.

ONE PLAY AWAY

By 1987, Burns had the Vikings back in the playoffs. He rotated two quarterbacks on offense, switching between experienced starter Tommy Kramer and the younger Wade Wilson. No matter who played under center, the top target was receiver Anthony Carter. At 5 feet, 11 inches and just 168 pounds, Carter looked physically overmatched on the field. But he was capable of big plays. In 1987, he averaged 24.3 yards per reception, leading the league.

After finishing 8–7, the Vikings traveled to New Orleans to face the Saints in the wild-card round. Sparked by a 44-yard Hail Mary touchdown from Wilson to receiver Hassan Jones on the last play of the first half, the Vikings won 44–10. It was the team's first playoff win in five years.

The next week, Minnesota went on the road again to face the powerhouse San Francisco 49ers.

Quarterback Tommy Kramer made 110 starts for the Vikings between 1977 and 1989. He threw 159 touchdown passes.

Wide receiver Anthony Carter's record for receiving yards in a playoff game stood until 1999.

Going against Jerry Rice, who many consider the greatest receiver ever, Carter stole the show. Though he didn't reach the end zone, the Vikings' star receiver caught 10 passes for a playoff-record 227 yards. His brilliant play contributed to a shocking 36–24 upset and put the Vikings in the NFC title game against Washington.

Once again underdogs, the Vikings hung in before falling behind 17–10 late in the fourth quarter. Wilson led Minnesota inside the Washington 10-yard line in the final minute. He lofted a pass to the goal line for running back Darrin Nelson, but it slipped through Nelson's hands, dooming the Vikings to defeat.

Defensive end Chris Doleman, *left*, and defensive tackle Keith Millard, *right*, led a fierce Vikings defense in the late 1980s and early 1990s.

THE TRADE

By 1989, the Vikings had once again built a dominant defense. Up front, defensive tackle Keith Millard won the NFL's Defensive Player of the Year Award. He finished the season with 18 sacks. That total would have been a team record, but defensive end Chris Doleman, a converted linebacker, had 21. If opponents managed to get past the defensive line, veteran linebacker Scott Studwell and strong safety Joey Browner were waiting to dish out punishing hits.

The Vikings' offense struggled to keep up. In an attempt to balance things out, general manager Mike Lynn pulled a major trade midway through the season. He sent a package of four players and eight future draft picks to the Dallas Cowboys for star running back Herschel Walker and three draft picks. It was the largest trade in the history of the league.

The deal turned into a huge disaster for the Vikings. Walker, considered the perfect combination of power and speed, never lived up to the hype in Minnesota. The Vikings lost their playoff opener in 1989 and missed the postseason altogether for the next two years, at which point Walker left the team. Meanwhile, Dallas used its haul of draft picks to build three Super Bowl–winning teams.

Receiver Cris Carter caught a team-record 1,004 passes in 12 seasons with the Vikings.

UNLIKELY STARS

In the wake of the deal for Walker, Burns had a tough job. With few top draft picks due to the trade, the Vikings had to find stars in other ways. Luckily, the Vikings had made a pair of shrewd moves in 1990. The first was picking up receiver Cris Carter from the Philadelphia Eagles. Carter had reliable hands and often made acrobatic catches look easy. But when he ran into problems off the field, the Eagles cut him. After the Vikings picked him up, Carter became the team's top receiver and built a Hall of Fame career. He also cleaned up his personal life, becoming an ordained minister and frequently mentoring Minnesota's younger players.

On defense, the Vikings signed defensive lineman John Randle as an undrafted free agent. After playing little his first year, the versatile Randle soon became one of the league's best pass rushers. He was also one of football's most entertaining players. Randle was known for his constant playful chatter on the field. And it wasn't always about the game. In one famous exchange, Randle yelled to a passing official, "Me and you should hang out! We should go fishing together!"

Defensive lineman John Randle recorded 137 1/2 sacks in his career.

A NEARLY PERFECT YEAR

Minnesota's new stars lined up for coach Dennis Green,

Dennis Green coached the Vikings from 1992 to 2001 and had only one losing season.

who took over for Burns in 1992. The passionate Green was one of the NFL's few Black head coaches. In his early years, the Vikings were competitive, but Minnesota struggled to break through as a real contender.

In Minnesota's opening game of the 1998 season, a rookie receiver gave fans a reason for excitement. The Vikings already led the Tampa Bay Buccaneers 7–0 when Randy Moss took off down the left sideline. Quarterback Brad Johnson heaved a pass Moss's way. Johnson underthrew the ball, but Moss battled his defender to make a juggling touchdown catch. On the Vikings' next drive, the pair connected on a 31-yard strike. Minnesota won 31–7, kicking off a magical season.

The Vikings featured a frightening offense in 1998. The team rolled up an NFL-record 556 points. Speedy runner Robert Smith used his long, graceful strides to chew up yards behind an offensive line anchored by Hall of Fame guard Randall McDaniel.

The Vikings drafted guard Randall McDaniel with the 19th pick of the 1988 draft. He starred for the team until 1999.

While the ground game was solid, the Vikings' passing game dominated. Carter remained one of the NFL's top receivers. Veteran Jake Reed provided a solid option for quarterbacks Johnson and Randall Cunningham. But Minnesota's biggest weapon was Moss.

The rookie receiver dropped to 21st in the draft after a checkered college career. He lost an opportunity to attend Notre Dame after getting arrested for fighting, and he got kicked out of Florida State for drug use. He ended up starring at Marshall University in West Virginia. The Vikings snapped him up, and he quickly began training in the offseason with Carter.

Receiver Randy Moss was named the Offensive Rookie of the Year in 1998.

Moss was so fast that few quarterbacks could throw the ball deep enough for him. But when passes were underthrown, Moss could stop on a dime and leap over helpless defensive backs. As a rookie, he caught 69 passes, led the team with 1,313 receiving yards, and led the NFL with 17 receiving touchdowns. Along the way, fans marveled at his speed and leaping ability.

The Vikings finished 15-1, the best record in team history, and rolled into the playoffs looking as if they would finally bring a championship to Minnesota. After thumping the Arizona Cardinals 41-21 in the divisional round, the Vikings hosted the 14-2 Atlanta Falcons in the NFC title game. Sparked by a 31-yard touchdown pass from Cunningham to Moss, the Vikings built a 20-7 lead. But the Falcons hung around. With the Vikings up 27-20 and 2:11 left, Minnesota's offense stalled at the Falcons' 22. Green sent out kicker Gary Anderson, who had been the team's secret weapon. The 39-year-old kicker had not missed a field goal or an extra-point kick all year. But Anderson's potential game-sealing field-goal attempt missed wide left. The Falcons then drove for a tying touchdown before beating the stunned Vikings 30-27 in overtime.

RANDY MOSS'S THANKSGIVING FEAST

Randy Moss vowed revenge on all the teams that didn't draft him. He saved his biggest moment for the Dallas Cowboys. When the teams met in a nationally televised game on Thanksgiving in 1998, Moss torched Dallas. He caught only three passes but racked up 163 yards. All three receptions were spectacular touchdowns in a 46-36 Minnesota win.

Vikings fans had been through many painful moments, but Anderson's missed kick devastated the team, coaches, and fans. "Gary hadn't missed one all year long," said offensive coordinator Brian Billick. "So I'm going back to the Gatorade thinking it's over. Then I hear the crowd groan, and I look up and see we had missed the field goal."

"I'M GOING BACK TO THE GATORADE THINKING IT'S OVER. THEN I HEAR THE CROWD GROAN, AND I LOOK UP AND SEE WE HAD MISSED THE FIELD GOAL."

—BRIAN BILLICK

The Vikings never recovered from the loss. The team returned to the NFC title game two years later, but the New York Giants crushed Minnesota 41–0. Over the coming seasons, the Vikings were unable to reach the heights of their amazing 1998 team. Many football observers consider it one of the best teams to never win the Super Bowl.

Kicker Gary Anderson watches from the turf as his field-goal attempt sails wide left in the NFC Championship Game after the 1998 season.

Running back Adrian Peterson jumps into the stands after scoring a touchdown against the San Diego Chargers in November 2007.

CHAPTER 5

MISHAPS AND MIRACLES

The Vikings entered Week 9 of the 2007 season struggling at 2–5. But fans still flocked to the Metrodome to see the team's newest star. Rookie running back Adrian "All Day" Peterson stood 6-foot-1 and weighed 220 pounds. With constantly churning legs, he powered through would-be tacklers. And when he found open space, he blasted off for long touchdowns.

Peterson already had four 100-yard games, including one 200-yard effort, by the time he took the field against the San Diego Chargers in Week 9. But through the first half, he had just 43 yards on 13 carries. Minnesota trailed 14–7 when Peterson broke loose for a 64-yard touchdown on the team's first drive of the second half. Throughout the final 30 minutes, Peterson kept pounding away. He added a 46-yard score in the fourth quarter to help the Vikings build a 35–17 lead.

With two minutes left, Peterson had 258 yards, which was 37 short of the single-game rushing record. The team decided to go for it. On the next play, Peterson took a handoff and cut back to the left, sprinting past three defenders for 35 yards. With the crowd chanting his initials, he finished off the record two plays later with a 3-yard plunge up the middle. All Day had run for 296 yards in all.

Peterson became the seventh running back to top 2,000 yards in a season when he rushed for 2,097 in 2012.

FROM MISSISSIPPI TO NEW ORLEANS

Peterson's thrilling runs were the top reason to watch the Vikings in the late 2000s. But head coach Brad Childress knew he needed a good quarterback to be competitive. The Vikings had reached the playoffs in 2008 only to watch young signal-caller Tarvaris Jackson complete just 15 of 35 passes in a loss. That August, a handful of the team's veteran players took a plane ride to Hattiesburg, Mississippi, the hometown of 40-year-old NFL legend Brett Favre. For years, Favre had tortured Vikings fans as the star quarterback of the rival Green Bay Packers.

Quarterback Brett Favre throws a pass against his former team, the Green Bay Packers, in 2009.

Favre had recently retired, and the Vikings flew down to talk him into coming back. Favre agreed and joined the Vikings just weeks before the 2009 season. Favre was famous for his risky style of quarterbacking. With his rocket arm, he could place accurate passes into the hands of receivers who didn't seem open. The downside to Favre's risk-taking was that he had also thrown more interceptions than any NFL quarterback. But for much of the 2009 season, everything Favre did seemed to go right. In Week 3, he showed off his thrilling style with a last-second, 32-yard touchdown pass to receiver Greg Lewis in double coverage to beat the San Francisco 49ers 27–24.

Favre put together one of his best seasons ever, throwing 33 touchdown passes and tossing a career-low seven interceptions. Meanwhile, Peterson led the NFL with 18 rushing touchdowns. The Vikings' defense was led by rugged pass rusher Jared Allen,

Defensive end Jared Allen had 85 1/2 sacks for the Vikings between 2008 and 2013.

Receiver Sidney Rice races in for one of his three touchdowns in the divisional playoffs against the Dallas Cowboys after the 2009 season.

who celebrated his 14 1/2 sacks with his signature dance in which he mimed roping a calf.

After finishing 12–4, Minnesota hosted the Dallas Cowboys in the divisional round. Dallas bottled up Peterson, holding the star rusher to just 63 yards. But the Cowboys had no answer for Favre and receiver Sidney Rice. The pair connected on a 47-yard touchdown pass late in the first quarter. They later hooked up for two more scores as the Vikings won 34–3.

That win sent Minnesota to New Orleans for an NFC title game matchup with the Saints. Late in a brutal game in which New Orleans defenders repeatedly thumped Favre, the teams were tied 28–28. Favre drove the Vikings to the Saints' 38 with 19 seconds left.

Minnesota was in range for a long field goal, but the offense tried one more play. Favre rolled right, then threw an interception. The Saints won 31–28 in overtime.

THE MIRACLE

On December 11, 2010, heavy snow fell in Minneapolis. So much accumulated on top of the Metrodome that the inflatable roof collapsed. With the field unusable, the Vikings had to find other spots for their last two games. The first was at Ford Field in Detroit. The second was played outdoors at the University of Minnesota.

The Metrodome was aging anyway, so the Vikings made plans to replace it. In 2014, the team began two years of outdoor home

Snow bursts through the roof of the Metrodome on the night of December 11, 2010.

Kicker Blair Walsh (3) misses his potential game-winning field goal against the Seattle Seahawks at the University of Minnesota's TCF Bank Stadium in January 2016.

games while they waited for their new home to be completed. It was a welcome callback to the team's frozen days at Metropolitan Stadium. Following the 2015 season, the Vikings took on the Seattle Seahawks in the wild-card round with temperatures at around −6 degrees Fahrenheit (−21°C). With seconds left, normally reliable Minnesota kicker Blair Walsh shanked a 27-yard field-goal attempt wide left, and the Vikings lost 10–9.

By 2016, those cold-weather games were once again a thing of the past. The Vikings moved into their sparkling new home at U.S. Bank Stadium. That season, Vikings fans developed a signature celebration called the Skol chant, slowly clapping their hands above

Vikings fans perform the Skol chant during a game against the Philadelphia Eagles in 2019.

their heads while yelling "Skol!" *Skol*, a traditional Scandinavian cheer, has been linked with the team since its earliest days.

The next year, Minnesota wasn't considered a contender, especially after quarterback Sam Bradford went down with an injury early in the season. But journeyman backup Case Keenum stepped in and connected well with Minnesota native Adam Thielen and explosive deep threat Stefon Diggs in the passing game. Under hard-nosed defensive-minded head coach Mike Zimmer, the Vikings blitzed their way to a surprising 13–3 record.

The Vikings hosted the Saints in the divisional round of the playoffs. Minnesota fans were itching for revenge from the NFC title game eight years earlier. In the years following the loss, the NFL discovered that the Saints' defense had been intentionally trying to injure opposing players with their hard hits. Because of the

A native of Detroit Lakes, Minnesota, receiver Adam Thielen caught 534 passes in nine years with the Vikings.

scandal, the NFL suspended Saints coach Sean Payton for the entire 2012 season.

Payton was back on the sideline in 2017, though, and he watched Minnesota build a 17–0 halftime lead. But the Saints battled back. With 3:01 left, New Orleans went up 21–20. The teams then traded late field goals, and when the Saints took a 24–23 lead with 25 seconds left, the game appeared over. Payton began taunting Vikings fans by doing the Skol clap on the sideline.

With 10 seconds to go, Minnesota faced third down at its own 39. The Saints backed off to defend against a deep pass. The Vikings' play call was named "Buffalo Right, Seven Heaven." It called for three receivers to run routes down the right side of the field. The Vikings hoped to gain enough yardage for a long field goal.

Diggs ran the deepest route, and Keenum heaved a pass that the receiver leaped to catch. As he did, New Orleans safety Marcus Williams dove for a crushing hit, but he missed Diggs completely. When the Vikings' receiver landed at the New Orleans 34, he steadied himself with his left hand and raced untouched to the end zone.

Receiver Stefon Diggs crosses the goal line to complete "the Minneapolis Miracle" in January 2018.

Quarterback Case Keenum waves to the fans as he leaves the field after the Minneapolis Miracle.

The stadium erupted, and the celebration lasted for several minutes. The stunned Saints had left the field, but the game could not officially end until the Vikings had tried an extra point. While the fans waited for 11 New Orleans players to straggle onto the field, Keenum led the fans in one last thunderous Skol chant. The quarterback then took a knee to finish off the 29–24 win. After the game, Keenum said to his teammates in the locker room, "Is this real life?"

> **"IS THIS REAL LIFE?"**
>
> **—CASE KEENUM**

A week after "the Minneapolis Miracle," the Vikings traveled to Philadelphia for the NFC title game. But the dream died when the Eagles routed Minnesota 38–7. Once again, the Vikings had come up just short of the league's biggest game.

VIKINGS TROPHY CASE

SUPER BOWL CHAMPIONSHIPS: 0

NFL CHAMPIONSHIPS: 1

1969

CONFERENCE CHAMPIONSHIPS: 4

1969, 1973, 1974, 1976

DIVISION TITLES: 21

NFL Central: 1968, 1969
NFC Central: 1970, 1971, 1973, 1974, 1975, 1976, 1977, 1978, 1980, 1989, 1992, 1994, 1998, 2000
NFC North: 2008, 2009, 2015, 2017, 2022

All stats are through the 2024 season.

MODERN LEGENDS

The Vikings made a big signing before the 2018 season, bringing in star quarterback Kirk Cousins to get the team over the top. Despite putting up big offensive numbers, the plan didn't work. The team's best season under Cousins came in 2022, when Minnesota finished 13–4 under new head coach Kevin O'Connell. The team specialized in close victories, winning a league-record 11 games decided by one score. Cousins left the team after the 2023 season, having delivered only one playoff win.

THE COMEBACK

Minnesota's most thrilling close call in 2022 came in Week 15. The team fell behind the Indianapolis Colts 33–0 at home. But led by four touchdown passes from quarterback Kirk Cousins, Minnesota battled back. The Vikings tied the game with 2:18 left when running back Dalvin Cook caught a screen pass and turned it into a 64-yard touchdown. Kicker Greg Joseph then won it 39–36 with a 40-yard field goal with three seconds left in overtime to complete the largest comeback in NFL history.

Despite that, the Vikings remained loaded with talent. Their biggest threat was superstar wide receiver Justin Jefferson. He combined with second-year wideout Jordan Addison and an aggressive defense to lead Minnesota to a 14–3 record in 2024. Once again, the Vikings came up short in the playoffs. Minnesota's long-suffering fans hoped that the team could soon build a strong enough roster to finally deliver a Super Bowl victory.

Justin Jefferson emerged as one of the league's very best wide receivers in the early 2020s.

TIMELINE

The Vikings win their opening game 37-13 over the Chicago Bears.
1961

1967
The Vikings hire Bud Grant, who coaches the team for 18 of the next 19 seasons.

Minnesota wins its first NFL title but falls to the Kansas City Chiefs in the Super Bowl on January 11.
1970

1974
The Vikings advance to the Super Bowl before losing 24-7 to the Miami Dolphins on January 13.

Minnesota reaches its second consecutive Super Bowl but loses 16-6 to the Pittsburgh Steelers on January 12.
1975

1977
The Vikings become the first team to lose four Super Bowls after falling 32-14 to the Oakland Raiders on January 9.

The Vikings reach the NFC title game but lose 17–10 to Washington on January 17.

1988

Adrian Peterson breaks the single-game rushing record, racking up 296 yards against the San Diego Chargers on November 4.

2007

Case Keenum and Stefon Diggs complete "the Minneapolis Miracle" on January 14 to send Minnesota to the NFC title game.

2018

1998

The Vikings set the NFL record for points in a season while finishing 15–1, but they fall short of the Super Bowl.

2010

Minnesota reaches the NFC title game but loses 31–28 in overtime to the New Orleans Saints on January 24.

2024

The Vikings finish the season with a strong 14–3 record, but they go on to lose in the first round of the playoffs.

GLOSSARY

blitz—when a linebacker or defensive back attacks the line of scrimmage to stop a run or sack the quarterback.

camaraderie—a sense of trust and friendship among teammates.

draft—a system that allows teams to acquire new players coming into a league.

expansion team—a new team that is added to an existing league.

free agent—a player who is not signed to a team.

general manager—an executive who runs a team and is responsible for finding and signing players.

Hail Mary—a long pass that has a small chance of succeeding, usually made near the end of a game as a last-ditch effort to score.

journeyman—a player who has played for many teams or has been unable to find a specific role.

mentor—to teach or train.

overtime—an extra period of play when the score is tied after regulation.

play-action— a play in which the quarterback fakes a handoff before dropping back to pass.

postseason—another word for playoffs; the time after the end of the regular season when teams play to determine a champion.

retire—to end one's career.

rival—an opponent with whom a player or team has a fierce and ongoing competition.

rookie—a professional athlete in his or her first year of competition.

sack—a tackle of the quarterback behind the line of scrimmage before he can pass the ball.

safety—a score of two points for a team when its opponent is unable to advance the ball out of its own end zone.

scandal—an action or event regarded as morally or legally wrong and causing general public outrage.

underdog—a person or team that is not expected to win.

veteran—someone who has played for many years.

wild-card—the first round of the playoffs.

ONLINE RESOURCES

To learn more about the Minnesota Vikings, please visit **abdobooklinks.com** or scan this QR code. These links are routinely monitored and updated to provide the most current information available.